DEATH AND RESURRECTION
OF
JESUS

by Frank Rinaldi

Six sessions for youth groups,
on Luke's Gospel

Bible Society

BIBLE SOCIETY
Stonehill Green, Westlea, SWINDON SN5 7DG, England

Photographs
Cover: © Jam Magazine, published by Scripture Union.
Page 8,11,15,20,23,27:   © ITC Entertainment Limited
Page 18:   A. Price, Ace Photo Agency
Page 12:   © Siegfried Eigstler
Page 13:   Reproduced by courtesy of Bemrose Calendars and Diaries, Derby (top), and the Trustees of the British
                             Museum (bottom)

First published 1988
Reprinted 1989

British Library Cataloguing in Publication Data
Rinaldi Frank
The death and resurrection of Jesus: 6 sessions for youth groups on Luke's Gospel – (Jesus series 3).
1. Jesus Christ
I. Title II. Series
232 BT301.9

ISBN 0 564 078328

Printed in Great Britain by Stanley L. Hunt (Printers) Ltd, Rushden, Northants
Designed by Belou Design Ltd, Stratford-upon-Avon

Bible Societies exist to provide resources for Bible distribution and use. Bible Society in England and Wales (BFBS) is a member of the United Bible Societies, an international partnership working in over 180 countries. Their common aim is to reach all people with the Bible, or some part of it, in a language they can understand and at a price they can afford. Parts of the Bible have now been translated into approximately 1,800 languages. Bible Societies aim to help every church at every point where it uses the Bible. You are invited to share in this work by your prayers and gifts. Bible Society in your country will be very happy to provide details of its activity.

Contents

How to use this book

out the group activities, then the leader's notes on page 30 will tell you more about what to do.

I think you will quickly find that exploring the Bible in this way can be entertaining and helpful. We all find reading the Bible on our own can be difficult, however, so the best approach would be to find some friends with whom you can meet to go through this book. You can then support each other as you explore the death and resurrection of Jesus.

...IN A GROUP

Some groups will have the same leader at every session, others will want to rotate the leadership. Some groups will be as small as three, others will be as large as twenty. Whatever your case, there are detailed leader's notes on pages 31-32, to ensure that sessions go smoothly.

Each group member will need a copy of this book, so make sure you buy enough to go round.

Being part of a group means more than just turning up at the meetings. What you put into these sessions will determine what you get out of them.

So to make the most of the group sessions, aim to read the passages before the session, and try out the Extra! project in the week following it. And come to each meeting prepared to listen to others and share your ideas and experiences. If everyone does that, this series of studies could have a great impact on individuals and the group.

...ON YOUR OWN

This book was designed for groups, but you can use it on your own if you make just a few changes.

All the sessions are based on Luke's Gospel, and at the back of this book (page 29) you will find a reading plan that takes you through the whole gospel in four weeks.

To do each Bible study you'll need a copy of this book, a Bible, a notebook, and a pen. Find somewhere quiet, and take one Bible study at a time. If you go through the book all in one go, you'll only get indigestion.

Read through the whole outline to start with. Mark with a cross any activity or questions you'd like to try out. You will soon see which parts will work only in a group. Even some of the warm-ups — for example, News (page 18) — you can try on your own. All you need is a supply of newspapers.

To make use of the discussion questions (marked ◈) simply write your thoughts in a notebook. When you come to the Bible passage, read it through twice and answer the questions that follow it. The Extra! is designed to be used on your own, so you'll have no trouble with this. If you want to try

Welcome to Luke's Gospel.

Luke is the longest of the four gospels. It shows us many things the other three do not. There are famous parables, such as the prodigal son and the good Samaritan. It is from Luke that we get the information about Jesus' mother and his home life. But it is Jesus the Saviour that is Luke's main theme. Luke 19.10 summarizes Luke's message: "The Son of Man came to seek and to save the lost."

Luke shows how Jesus brings people hope. The miracles, the parables, and the teachings all reach a climax as Jesus heads for Jerusalem to finish the work he began three years earlier, in Galilee. And although Luke's Gospel finishes with Jesus' ascension, the writer does not stop there. His gospel is, in fact, the first part of a two-part work. Luke's second book − Acts − picks up the story where his gospel ends.

Luke writes his gospel to "Theophilus" − see chapter 1, verse 1. The name "Theophilus" in fact means "friend of God", and people have wondered whether Luke meant by this that his gospel was written for anyone who wanted to find out about Jesus Christ.

Others think "Theophilus" might have been a real person − an important Gentile, interested in finding out more about the Christian faith. But whoever "Theophilus" was supposed to be, most people agree that Luke intended his book for the Greek-speaking world − i.e. for the people who did not have much background in the stories of the Old Testament. The writer Luke seems to have been a Gentile rather than a Jew. And from medical words he uses in his work, some people think that he may have been a doctor.

Luke probably wrote about thirty years after Jesus' death and resurrection, while many of the eyewitnesses of those momentous events were still alive.

INTO JERUSALEM

AIM: To explore how Jesus followed God's plan for him.

WARM UP

MY AIM IN LIFE...

How well do you know the others in this group? How well do they know you? Let's find out.

On the bottom of a sheet of paper, simply write your name. Then hand it to the person on your right.

Now look at the sheet you've been handed. Check whose name is at the bottom. Think how that person might finish this sentence; "My aim in life is...", in not more than ten words. If it's someone whom you don't know at all, you'll have to make an inspired guess. Write it down on the paper. Then fold the paper to just hide what you have written. Now pass it to the person on your right.

Repeat this process until your paper comes back to you. Now read through what people have written on your sheet. Pick out two sentences — one that is furthest from , and one that is nearest to, the truth.

Now a few volunteers read out their two chosen sentences.

These six sessions pick up the story of Jesus where he is ready to enter Jerusalem.

Read the following two passages.

JESUS SPEAKS A THIRD TIME ABOUT HIS DEATH

31 Jesus took the twelve disciples aside and said to them, "Listen! We are going to Jerusalem where everything the prophets wrote about the Son of Man will come true. 32He will be handed over to the Gentiles, who will mock him, insult him, and spit on him. 33They will whip him and kill him, but three days later he will rise to life."

34 But the disciples did not understand any of these things; the meaning of the words was hidden from them, and they did not know what Jesus was talking about.
(LUKE 18.31-34)

...35and they took the colt to Jesus. Then they threw their cloaks over the animal and helped Jesus get on. 36As he rode on, people spread their cloaks on the road.

37 When he came near Jerusalem, at the place where the road went down the Mount of Olives, the large crowd of his disciples began to thank God and praise him in loud voices for all the great things that they had seen: 38"God bless the king who comes in the name of the Lord! Peace in heaven and glory to God!"

39 Then some of the Pharisees in the crowd spoke to Jesus. "Teacher," they said, "command your disciples to be quiet!"

40 Jesus answered, "I tell you that if they keep quiet, the stones themselves will start shouting."
(LUKE 19.35-40)

DISCUSS:

◇ Is it important to have an aim in life?
◇ Why/why not?

SPOT CHECK

On the first passage:

1. What does this passage say Jesus' reasons are for going to Jerusalem?
2. What does it tell us about Jesus' understanding of himself?

On the second passage:

3. Look at the different people in the story. How do you think they were feeling? Match a mood with the people.

Jesus	**Angry**
	Sad
Disciples	**Suspicious**
	In a party mood
Crowd	**Somber**
Pharisees	**Puzzled**
	Determined

4. How would you explain the reason for their moods?

OVER TO YOU

1. Is there anything in this passage that you don't understand and would like explained?
2. Is there anything else in this passage you want to discuss before moving on?

BACKGROUND

◆Jesus was going to Jerusalem for the feast of the Passover. This was one of the great festivals of the Jewish year, when the people reminded themselves of the dramatic way in which God had saved them from the Egyptians, (read Exodus 12). It was a time of fun and excitement, when large numbers of people came to Jerusalem. It was also a time when patriotic feeling was at its highest. It was thought that God's promised Messiah would appear at Passover in Jerusalem.

◆Although there was a price on his head Jesus didn't slip into the city unnoticed. He came in openly. The way he came was important. He chose to fulfil an Old Testament prophecy (Zechariah 9.9-10). This said that one day a king would come to Jerusalem riding on a donkey. Donkeys were the common means of transport. Horses, on the other hand, were military animals. If Jesus had ridden in on a horse, it could have been taken as a sign for a military uprising against the Romans.

WORK OUT 1

PROTEST

In these passages we see people failing to understand the real meaning of Jesus' actions. The same happens today. People don't always see the true meaning of religious events.

Imagine it's Easter time. All around you people are getting ready to enjoy the "holiday".

Get into pairs to write a "protest" letter to the local paper, to put the record straight. Explain to the readers in your own way what the real meaning of Easter is.

To the Editor – The Evening News
Dear Editor

Yours faithfully

DISCUSS:

✧How could you help to make people more aware of the meaning of Easter?

WORK OUT 2

What does Jesus mean to you?

On your own, write in the space below five or more words that you would use to describe Jesus.

_____

_____

_____

_____

_____

Now choose just one of them. Join a partner and tell them the word you have chosen.

All together again, write everyone's chosen words onto a large poster.

EXTRA!

People today misunderstand the words and actions of Jesus in many different ways. Some people, for example, think God wants us to be unhappy. Others think that Christianity is all about "Thou shalt not...".

In the coming week, watch out for any other misunderstandings people have about Christianity and note them down here. _____

_____

_____

_____

_____

_____

Also bring along to the next session a gift or present you have been given, and which you particularly value.

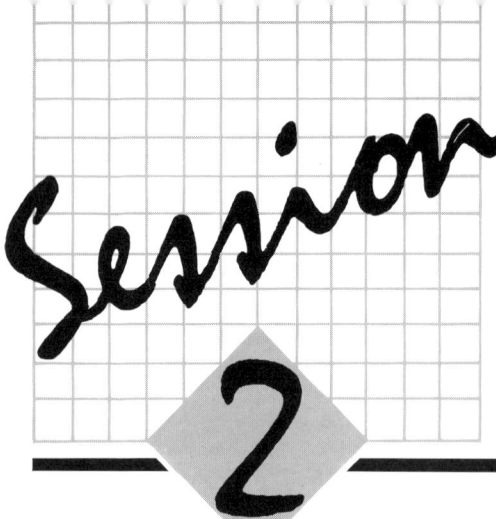

THE LAST SUPPER

AIM: To see how Jesus gave his disciples gifts to remember him by.

WARM UP

GIFTS

Everyone should have brought with them a present or gift they've received.

Put the gifts together in the centre of the room. Now quickly guess whom each of the gifts belongs to.

When everyone has guessed, each person who's brought a gift should show theirs to the rest of the group, and say why it is important to them.

DISCUSS:

◈What makes a gift important to us?

WORK IN

In the following passage we see Jesus giving two important gifts to his disciples.

Jesus takes a familiar festival, and gives the symbols in it new meaning. He uses the Passover meal as a sort of "visual aid".

Read the passage as a play. You will need a narrator and Jesus.

THE LORD'S SUPPER

14 When the hour came, Jesus took his place at the table with the apostles. ¹⁵He said to them, "I have wanted so much to eat this Passover meal with you before I suffer! ¹⁶For I tell you, I will never eat it until it is given its full meaning in the Kingdom of God."

17 Then Jesus took a cup, gave thanks to God, and said, "Take this and share it among yourselves. ¹⁸I tell you that from now on I will not drink this wine until the Kingdom of God comes."

19 Then he took a piece of bread, gave thanks to God, broke it, and gave it to them, saying, "This is my body, which is given for you. Do this in memory of me." ²⁰In the same way, he gave them the cup after the supper, saying, "This cup is God's new covenant sealed with my blood, which is poured out for you.

21 "But look! The one who betrays me is here at the table with me! ²²The Son of Man will die as God has decided, but how terrible for that man who betrays him!"

23 Then they began to ask among themselves which one of them it could be who was going to do this.
(LUKE 22.14-23)

SPOT CHECK

1. What two gifts does Jesus give his disciples? (Described here as apostles.)
2. What did they stand for?
3. Jesus speaks about wanting to eat the meal "before I suffer". What do you think this means?

OVER TO YOU

1. How would you describe the atmosphere in the room?

☐ Relaxed

☐ Tense

☐ Mournful

☐ Expectant

Tick one, and explain your answer.

2. Is there anything in this passage that you don't understand and would like explained?
3. Is there anything else in this passage you want to discuss before moving on?

BACKGROUND

◆Bread and wine were the familiar elements of the annual Passover meal. At this meal the Jewish people celebrated the night that God had set the people free from slavery.

◆The bread also has added significance. Bread played an important part in Jewish worship. It was offered along with the sacrifices. There was a "Feast of Unleavened Bread" which had links with the Passover. It is described in Exodus 12.34-39; 13.3-10. Bread was taken as a sign that God provides for his people. Jesus had earlier identified himself and his work with bread (John 6.25-59).

◆Covenant means promise, or agreement. In the biblical sense, a covenant is a relationship between God and his people. It is based on certain conditions or promises. The people's promise was to obey and keep God's law (Exodus 24.1-8). The problem was that God's people never kept their part of the agreement. What Jesus is saying, is that through his death he was making possible a new kind of covenant — a new kind of relationship between man and God.

WORK OUT 1

REMEMBER ME

Jesus gave three gifts at the Last Supper so that his disciples would remember him. Many of us have short memories, and we need constantly reminding of the important things in life.

Imagine you have been asked to create a calendar which will hang in your home – in the living room, the kitchen, or in a bedroom – which aims to remind people of Jesus.

Each page should show the days of the month etc., as all calendars do. But in addition draw (or choose) a picture, and a text from the Gospel of Luke, which you would like people to be reminded of each day.

When the pages are finished, staple them together and (if it's good enough) consider auctioning the calendar to the highest bidder, to boost your group funds.

DISCUSS:

✪ What other things help us remember Jesus from day to day?

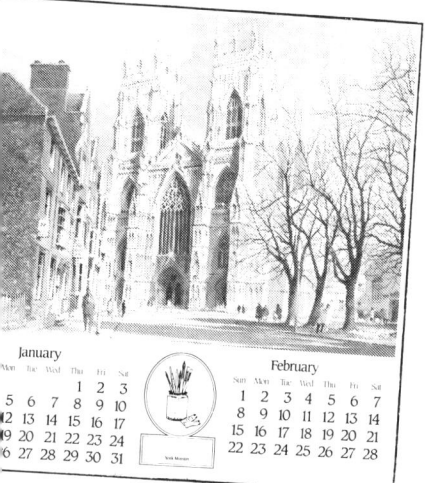

Jesus said that one of the disciples would betray him — see verse 21.

Write below your own definition of the word "betray".

_____

_____

_____

_____

_____

DISCUSS:

◈ In what way did the disciples betray Jesus?

◈ In what ways do we betray Jesus today?

▶ EXTRA!

At New Year we often make resolutions. Some of them last longer than others. It may not be New Year, but are there any resolutions that you would like to make that would help you to remember Jesus better from day to day?

Write them below, and then make them the subject of your prayers this week.

_____

_____

_____

_____

_____

_____

_____

_____

_____

_____

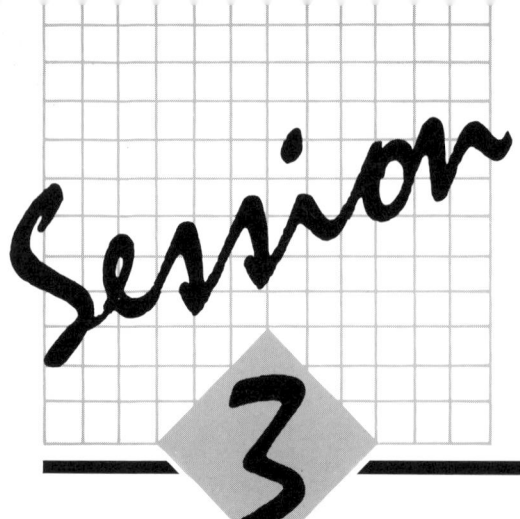

THE TRIAL

AIM: To see why Jesus, although innocent, was found guilty.

STANDING FIRM

Get into pairs. One of you is x, the other is y.

Xs choose a particularly unusual and dangerous pet you've decided to keep — for example a poisonous spider, or a killer whale. Your partner has one minute to dissuade you from keeping that dangerous pet.

Now swap around. Ys think of a particularly dangerous or unusual hobby you've decided to take up — for example skiing down Mount Everest, or collecting Cruise missiles! Your partner has one minute to dissuade you from this course of action.

DISCUSS:

✦ Do you ever get persuaded to do things against your better judgement?

WORK IN

In a game, it's easy to stand your ground. In real life it's more difficult. In today's passage we see how Pilate took a decision about Jesus that was based not on what he really believed, but on pressure from those around him.

Read through the passage. Take parts. You will need a Narrator and Pilate. The rest of the group read the part of the Crowd.

JESUS IS SENTENCED TO DEATH

13 Pilate called together the chief priests, the leaders, and the people, ¹⁴and said to them, "You brought this man to me and said that he was misleading the people. Now, I have examined him here in your presence, and I have not found him guilty of any of the crimes you accuse him of. ¹⁵Nor did Herod find him guilty, for he sent him back to us. There is nothing this man has done to deserve death. ¹⁶So I will have him whipped and let him go." *

18 The whole crowd cried out, "Kill him! Set Barabbas free for us!" (¹⁹Barabbas had been put in prison for a riot that had taken place in the city, and for murder.)

20 Pilate wanted to set Jesus free, so he appealed to the crowd again. ²¹But they shouted back, "Crucify him! Crucify him!"

22 Pilate said to them the third time, "But what crime has he committed? I cannot find anything he has done to deserve death! I will have him whipped and set him free."

23 But they kept on shouting at the top of their voices that Jesus should be crucified, and finally their shouting succeeded. ²⁴So Pilate passed the sentence on Jesus that they were asking for.
(LUKE 23.13-24)

* Some old documents add verse 17 as an explanation of Pilate's action: "At every Passover Festival Pilate had to set free one prisoner for them."

SPOT CHECK

1. What was the charge against Jesus? (see also Luke 23.1-3.)
2. Is there anything to show that Jesus was:
   - ☐ Guilty
   - ☐ Innocent
3. What does Pilate seem to think of Jesus?

OVER TO YOU

1. Is there anything in this passage that you don't understand and would like explained?
2. Is there anything else in this passage you want to discuss before moving on?

BACKGROUND

◆Pilate was a Roman official, the governor of Judaea.

◆Death by crucifixion was a punishment practised by the Phoenicians and the Persians, and adopted by the Romans. It was used for slaves and foreigners, not Romans. To the Jew it was the ultimate disgrace — it was a public demonstration of servitude. Even more, it brought God's curse on all who suffered it.

WORK OUT 1

INNOCENT!

Three volunteers will be needed, to try out a role-play.

The situation: some graffiti has been found on a wall at school. The teacher has asked the person who was responsible to own up, otherwise the whole class will be punished.

A. You did the graffiti but you have no intention of owning up, even if the whole class get punished. In fact you intend that B should get the blame. B always gets the blame for things.

B. You don't know who did the graffiti, but it wasn't you. You can feel the anger of the class if they all get punished.
C. You saw A doing the graffiti, but you are scared of A. A knows you know, and has threatened you with "trouble" if you tell the teacher.

Allow a few minutes for the characters to try to resolve the situation.

DISCUSS:

✧ Have people ever put the blame on you, when you're innocent?
✧ How did it feel?
✧ How do you think Jesus felt?

WORK OUT 2

Look up Luke 22.31-34 and 54-62. Like Pilate, Peter was swayed by the hostile crowd. The same can happen to us.

1. How would you handle any hostility that comes from being one of Jesus' followers?

   - ☐ **Very well**
   - ☐ **Well**
   - ☐ **Not too well**
   - ☐ **Poorly**

Tick one, and explain your answer.

....
....
....
....
....
....
....
....
....

2. What kind of hostility do you find most difficult to cope with?

☐ **Anger**
☐ **Disinterest**
☐ **Being put-down**
☐ **Mockery**

DISINTEREST

ANGER

MOCKERY

PUT DOWN

DISCUSS:

◈ What's the best way of dealing with each sort of hostility?

EXTRA!

Read Luke 23.1-12. Can you think of three reasons why Jesus was able to handle the hostility as calmly as he did?

1. ....
2. ....
3. ....

To think through – how can Jesus' example help us to handle hostility?

THE CRUCIFIXION

AIM: To discover why the death of Jesus is important for us today.

 **WARM UP**

NEWS

In groups of three, look through some newspapers for stories or articles about people who have helped others.

Particularly look for ones where people did it at some cost or danger to themselves. Maybe they made a sacrifice, or suffered in the process.

Cut out the stories you find, and paste them onto a sheet of paper.

If you can think of other stories not in the papers, but which you've heard about, write the the main details onto the sheet.

Share what you have found with the rest of the group.

DISCUSS:

◈ Do you think you would act in the same way in such situations?

P.C. Pat Abrams rescued from the sea. He had been trying to save a man who had tried to rescue a dog.

WORK IN

In this passage the events surrounding the death of Jesus are brought to a climax, as Luke show us Jesus dying on the cross. Have two readers:

Reader 1, read Luke 23.32-43; Reader 2, read Luke 23.44-49.

32 Two other men, both of them criminals, were also led out to be put to death with Jesus. 33When they came to the place called "The Skull," they crucified Jesus there, and the two criminals, one on his right and the other on his left. 34Jesus said, "Forgive them, Father! They don't know what they are doing."

They divided his clothes among themselves by throwing dice. 35The people stood there watching while the Jewish leaders jeered at him: "He saved others; let him save himself if he is the Messiah whom God has chosen!"

36 The soldiers also mocked him: they came up to him and offered him cheap wine, 37and said, "Save yourself if you are the king of the Jews!"

38 Above him were written these words: "This is the King of the Jews."

39 One of the criminals hanging there hurled insults at him: "Aren't you the Messiah? Save yourself and us!"

40 The other one, however, rebuked him, saying "Don't you fear God? You received the same sentence he did. 41Ours, however, is only right, because we are getting what we deserve for what we did; but he has done no wrong." 42And he said to Jesus, "Remember me, Jesus, when you come as King!"

43 Jesus said to him, "I promise you that today you will be in Paradise with me."

(LUKE 23.32-43)

THE DEATH OF JESUS

44 It was about twelve o'clock when the sun stopped shining and darkness covered the whole country until three o'clock; 45and the curtain hanging in the Temple was torn in two. 46Jesus cried out in a loud voice, "Father! In your hands I place my spirit!" He said this and died.

47 The army officer saw what had happened, and he praised God, saying, "Certainly he was a good man!"

48 When the people who had gathered there to watch the spectacle saw what happened, they all went back home, beating their breasts in sorrow. 49All those who knew Jesus personally, including the women who had followed him from Galilee, stood at a distance to watch.

(LUKE 23.44-49)

SPOT CHECK

First passage:

1. How did the two people crucified with Jesus react to him?
2. What do you think Jesus meant by his promise to one of the men?
3. Why did people say Jesus could have saved himself?

Second passage:

1. What do Jesus' words in verse 46 tell us about his attitude?
2. Who saw Jesus die?
3. How did they respond?
4. Why did they respond in this way?

OVER TO YOU

1. Take a verse from either passage that seems important to you, and put it into your own words.
2. Is there anything in this passage that you don't understand and would like explained?
3. Is there anything else in the passage you want to discuss before moving on?

BACKGROUND

◆It was thought at the time of Jesus that important events were accompanied by some sign or dramatic event. The eclipse of the sun would be seen as such an event.
◆Behind the curtain was the holiest part of the Temple. It was understood that God was specially present in this place. Once a year the High Priest was allowed to go in — on his own. When the curtain was torn, verse 45, is was a sign that the way to God was now open to everyone.

WORK OUT 1

WHY DID JESUS DIE?

Together, read Isaiah 53.1-12.

You have been asked by your church leaders to create a poster for display on the church notice board at Easter, called "Why did Jesus die?". Using the passages read in this session (Luke 23.32-43,44-49, and Isaiah 53.1-12) create a poster which expresses why you think Jesus died, and what his death achieved for us.

Get into groups of three or four. Decide together how you would finish the sentence "Jesus died to...", or "Jesus died so...", in about ten words.

Then using pictures from magazines, and the other art materials available, make a poster.

When the posters are finished, explain yours to the rest of the group.

DISCUSS:

◈ Do you think people understand the meaning of the death of Jesus?
◈ How could you help them to understand better?

WORK OUT 2

We finish this session by listening to different pieces of music which try to capture the mood of these events.

After listening to them, say which you liked most, and why.

DISCUSS:

◈ What kind of music would you have chosen to express the death of Jesus?

EXTRA!

Luke tells us that Jesus came "to seek and to save the lost". He was so concerned about us that he gave his life for us, and died instead of us.

What God wants is that we should give our lives to him in return. This week consider making a promise to God, or confirming the promise already made, that you will give your life to him.

Write your promise in the space below, and use it as a prayer this week. Sign it, to remind yourself of the promise you have made to God.

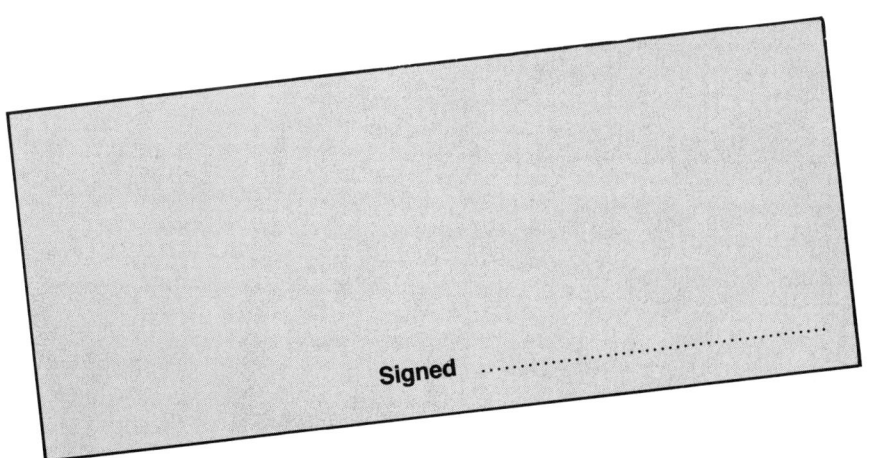

Signed ....

THE EMPTY TOMB

AIM: To look at the first reactions to the resurrection of Jesus.

 WARM UP

MAJOR EVENT

Each of you think of a major event in your life — something exciting, dangerous, scaring, exhilarating, or significant.

It should be something that you'll remember for the rest of your life and which, if you were looking back in years to come, you would say helped to make you the sort of person you are now.

Get together with a partner and share your "major event" with them.

Then, together again as a group, tell the rest about your partner's "major event".

DISCUSS:

◈Do we see any one differently as a result of those experiences?

WORK IN

This passage concerns not only a major event in the life of the disciples, but the main event that has influenced not just the life of the disciples, but world history.

Read through the passage, which describes the disciples' very first reactions to the resurrection.

THE RESURRECTION

Very early on Sunday morning the women went to the tomb, carrying the spices they had prepared. [2]They found the stone rolled away from the entrance to the tomb, [3]so they went in; but they did not find the body of the Lord Jesus. [4]They stood there puzzled about this, when suddenly two men in bright shining clothes stood by them. [5]Full of fear the women bowed down to the ground, as the men said to them, "Why are you looking among the dead for one who is alive? [6]He is not here; he has been raised. Remember what he said to you while he was in Galilee: [7]"The Son of Man must be handed over to sinful men, be crucified, and three days later rise to life."

8 Then the women remembered his words, [9]returned from the tomb, and told all these things to the eleven disciples and all the rest. [10]The women were Mary Magdalene, Joanna, and Mary the mother of James; they and the other women with them told these things to the apostles. [11]But the apostles thought that what the women said was nonsense and they did not believe them. [12]But Peter got up and ran to the tomb; he bent down and saw the linen wrappings but nothing else. Then he went back home amazed at what had happened.
(LUKE 24.1-12)

SPOT CHECK

1. Why were the women going to the tomb?
2. What was their first reaction when they found it empty?
3. How was Peter's response different from the rest?

OVER TO YOU

1. What was your response when you first heard the story of the resurrection?

   ☐ It's nonsense
   ☐ It's doubtful
   ☐ It's possible
   ☐ It makes sense
   ☐ Other ....

   (Tick one, and explain your answer.)

2. Has your opinion changed now? If so why, and how?
3. Is there anything in this passage that you don't understand and would like explained?
4. Is there anything else in this passage you want to discuss before moving on?

BACKGROUND

◆Spices were sweet smelling plants, seeds, and oils. They were highly valued and used for a number of purposes, such as the preparation of bodies for burial. John 19.39 tells us that Nicodemus provided about thirty kilogrammes of "a mixture of myrrh and aloes" for the burial of Jesus.
◆In the middle-east, tombs were often carved out of rock and bodies laid in a shelf inside. The tomb was closed with a very large stone. When the women came, this stone had already been rolled away.
◆Luke links three important occasions in the life of Jeus by the appearance of two men. The transfiguration (Luke 9.30), the resurrection, and the ascension (Acts 1.10). The first readers would have understood from their sudden appearance and the way that they were dressed that these were messengers from God, or angels.

WORK OUT 1

IN THE SPOTLIGHT

Many people find the resurrection hard to believe. They look for other explanations of the empty tomb. Let's see how some of these other explanations stand up to questioning.

Split into pairs. Each pair take one of the following theories or explanations of the empty tomb.

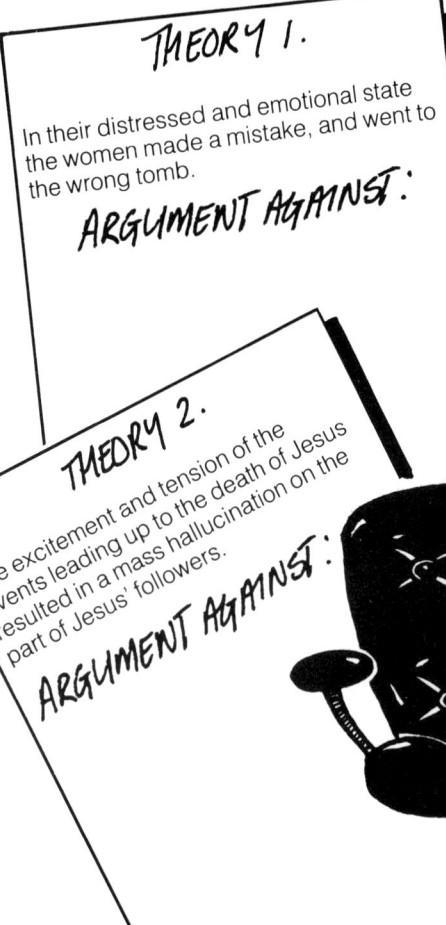

THEORY 1.

In their distressed and emotional state the women made a mistake, and went to the wrong tomb.

ARGUMENT AGAINST:

THEORY 2.

The excitement and tension of the events leading up to the death of Jesus resulted in a mass hallucination on the part of Jesus' followers.

ARGUMENT AGAINST:

You will have a few minutes to work out why that theory is reasonable. Be prepared to defend it. After that, each pair will go under the spotlight and be questioned about their theory.

DISCUSS:

⬦Why do you think that the tomb was empty?

THEORY 3.

Jesus did not really die! Due to weakness and loss of blood he passed out, or went into a deep coma, which was mistaken for death. Later, in the coolness of the tomb, he recovered and made his escape.

ARGUMENT AGAINST:

THEORY 4.

Jesus' body was stolen by either the disciples, the Jews, or Romans.

ARGUMENT AGAINST:

WORK OUT 2

What finally convinced those first followers that Jesus had risen from the dead, was meeting with the risen Lord.

Do you know how many people saw him alive?

Get into the same pairs as for the last activity. Each of you will be given a Bible passage to look up and explore.

Look up your passage, and try to identify three things about it:

◆Where were the people when they saw Jesus alive?
◆Roughly how many people saw him?
◆What was their reaction?

Note down your answers to these three questions, then get back together again with the rest of the group. Display your findings on a large chart.

DISCUSS:

⬦ Why is it difficult to convince people of the truth of the resurrection today?
⬦ Why is the resurrection so important for Christians?

EXTRA!

Someone asks you, "How do you know Jesus rose from the dead?"

Write down as many reasons as you can.

_____

_____

_____

_____

_____

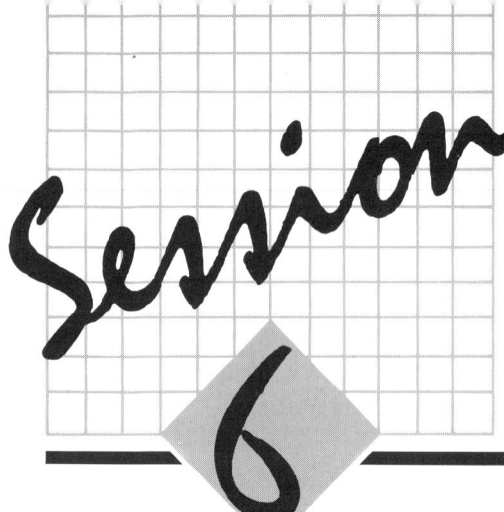

JESUS IS ALIVE!

AIM: To see how Jesus equipped his disciples for his departure.

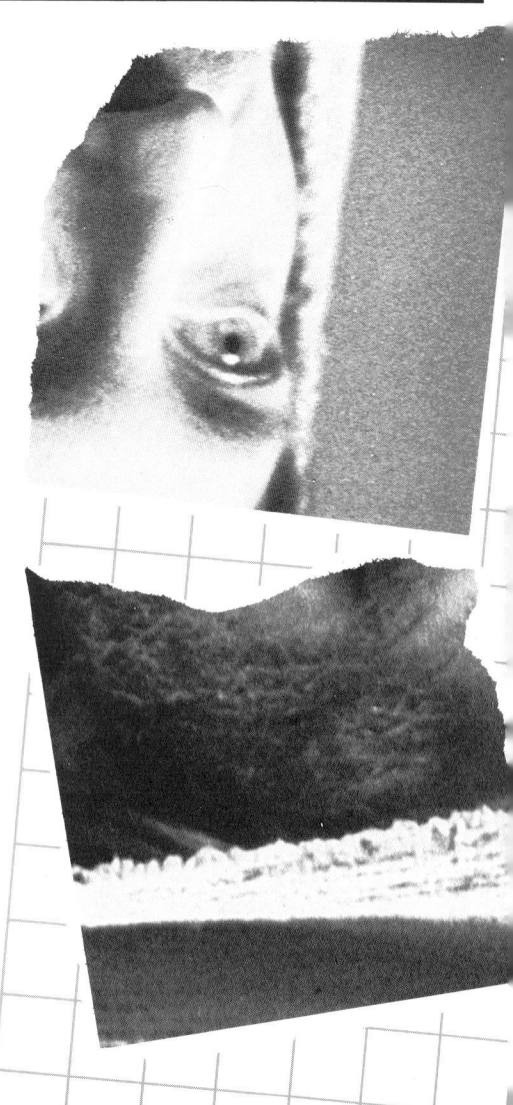

WARM UP

THE COMPLETE PICTURE

Together, attempt to piece together the cut-up pictures that are in the envelopes.

WORK IN

Now read Luke 24.36-49. In this passage we see the final pieces in the "Jesus jigsaw" being put into place. As Jesus appears to his disciples, he prepares them for his departure. Now the events of the past three years begin to make sense to the disciples.

JESUS APPEARS TO HIS DISCIPLES

36 While the two were telling them this, suddenly the Lord himself stood among them and said to them, "Peace be with you."

37 They were terrified, thinking that they were seeing a ghost. 38But he said to them, "Why are you alarmed? Why are these doubts coming up in your minds? 39Look at my hands and my feet and see that it is I myself. Feel me, and you will know, for a ghost doesn't have flesh and bones, as you can see I have."

40 He said this and showed them his hands and his feet. 41They still could not believe, they were so full of joy and wonder; so he asked them, "Have you anything here to eat?" 42They gave him a piece of cooked fish, 43which he took and ate in their presence.

44 Then he said to them, "These are the very things I told you about while I was still with you; everything written about me in the Law of Moses, the writings of the prophets, and the Psalms had to come true."

45 Then he opened their minds to understand the Scriptures, 46and said to them, "This is what is written: the Messiah must suffer and must rise from death three days later, 47and in his name the message about repentance and the forgiveness of sins must be preached to all nations, beginning in Jerusalem. 48You are witnesses of these things. 49And I myself will send upon you what my Father has promised. But you must wait in the city until the power from above comes down upon you."
(LUKE 24.36-49)

SPOT CHECK

1. What did Jesus do to help them realize that he was not a ghost?
2. What task was given to the disciples?
3. What did it involve?
4. What did Jesus promise them?

OVER TO YOU

1. What would you say to someone who said that the whole thing was an hallucination, or that it was a ghost?
2. Is there anything in this passage that you don't understand and would like explained?
3. Is there anything else in this passage you want to discuss before moving on?

BACKGROUND

◆At the time when Luke was writing, there were people who had begun to teach that the body of the risen Jesus only seemed to be real. Luke points out the physical nature of the resurrection. Jesus is not a ghost – he eats, he can be touched. The flesh-and-blood Jesus and the risen Jesus are the same.

◆Luke wrote a sequel to his gospel – the Acts of the Apostles – which takes up where this leaves off, and tells what happened to the disciples.

 **WORK OUT 1**

ALL NATIONS

Jesus gave his disciples specific instructions on what to do when he went away. They were to wait in Jerusalem until they received the Holy Spirit, then they were to go out with his message and spread it to all nations.

That is part of our role as Christians today. Let's see how we might go about doing that.

Get into groups of three. From the pictures provided, choose two pictures which could be used to illustrate a situation in which Christians could help spread God's message.

Imagine you could make the picture into a poster. Write a caption which would attract the reader and inspire them to help spread God's message in this situation.

DISCUSS:

✦ In which of these situations do you think you might be able to best spread God's message?

 **WORK OUT 2**

Looking back over the past six sessions – or the past twelve if you have also used the earlier book, "The life of Jesus" – what thing has most stood out for you about Jesus?

Write your ideas here:

Find a partner, and explain your ideas to them.

Then all together again, pray for each other, that Jesus' power will continue to make each of us more like him and more able to do his will, whatever the situation we find ourselves in.

 **EXTRA!**

Find out what happened to those early followers of Jesus.

If you've already read through the whole of Luke's Gospel (there's a reading plan on the next page if you haven't), start to read the second part of Luke's story – the book of Acts.

LUKE'S GOSPEL READING PLAN

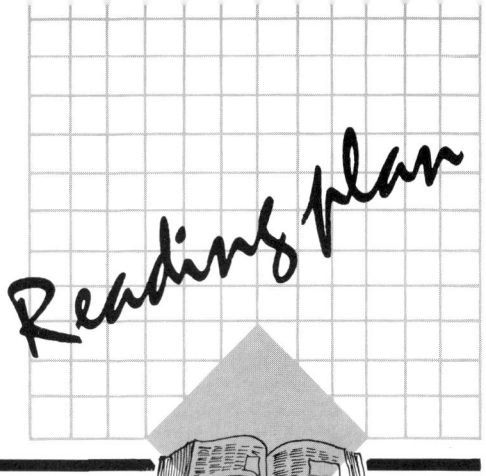

Have you thought about reading all through Luke's Gospel? The best approach would be to read it straight through, as if it were a novel. But if you want it broken up, this is a plan which will take you through it in just over one month. Tick the passages off as you read them.

Introductions
DAY 1 Why Luke wrote his gospel. Zechariah is told about John the Baptist's birth. *1.1-25*
DAY 2 Mary is told about Jesus' birth. *1.26-56*
DAY 3 The birth of John the Baptist. *1.57-80*
DAY 4 The birth of Jesus. *2.1-40*
DAY 5 Jesus' childhood. *2.41-52*

Jesus prepares for his public work
DAY 6 John the Baptist prepares the way. *3.1-20*
DAY 7 The baptism and ancestors of Jesus. *3.21-38*
DAY 8 The temptation of Jesus. *4.1-13*

The public work of Jesus
DAY 9 Powerful words. Powerful actions. *4.14-5.26*
DAY 10 Jesus chooses his followers. *5.27-6.16*
DAY 11 A summary of his teaching. *6.17-49*
DAY 12 His powerful effect on others. *7.1-35*
DAY 13 Women in his ministry. *7.36-8.3*
DAY 14 The purpose of parables. *8.4-21*
DAY 15 Jesus has power over all things. *8.22-56*
DAY 16 The purpose of Jesus' ministry. *9.1-27*

DAY 17 The climax of his ministry. *9.28-50*

Jesus on the way to Jerusalem
DAY 18 Getting his followers ready. *9.51-10.24*
DAY 19 General teaching. *10.25-13.21*
DAY 20 Conflict with the authorities. *13.22-16.31*
DAY 21 Teaching the disciples. *17.1-18.30*

Events leading to the death of Jesus
DAY 22 The journey to Jerusalem. *18.31-19.27*
DAY 23 The entry into Jerusalem. *19.28-44*
DAY 24 Teaching in Jerusalem *19.45-21.4*
DAY 25 Teaching about signs of the times. *21.5-38*
DAY 26 The last supper. *22.1-38*
DAY 27 Jesus is betrayed. *22.39-62*
DAY 28 The arrest and trial. *22.63-23.25*
DAY 29 The death of Jesus. *23.26-56*

The resurrection
DAY 30 The empty tomb and walk to Emmaus. *24.1-35*
DAY 31 The appearance to the disciples. *24.36-43*
DAY 32 The great commission and the ascension. *24.44-53*

Six one-hour sessions explore the death and resurrection of Jesus. It's a big subject for a short book, so it's worth saying right from the start:

◆This book is one of a pair. It picks up where the earlier volume, **The life of Jesus**, ended. It's difficult to appreciate the significance of "Holy week" without looking at Jesus' life, and vice versa. So do all you can to use the other volume, too.

◆There isn't space or time to read all of the Holy week passages together, as a group. Some might do so on their own, but not everyone. So this book can only offer glimpses of the full meaning of Jesus' death and resurrection. But if at the end people are left wanting to find out more, then I'll feel well pleased.

YOUR ROLE

What kind of person makes a good small group leader? Certainly someone who is:

◆Open and honest
◆Non-manipulative
◆In touch with their own feelings, including the negative ones
◆Teachable, as well as able to teach

But a leader also has three overlapping tasks:

◆To be aware of the needs of individuals, and help them
◆To be aware of what's going on in the group and to help if, for example, discussion is getting bogged down
◆To help the group keep to the task set, and so to get the most out of the study

The notes that follow are to help you in all those tasks, and so to help you lead with confidence and excitement.

If you are unsure how you are doing as a leader, an evaluation sheet can help. Try, for example, putting the following questions on a form, and handing them round at the end of a session:

◆In this group the most helpful things were......
◆The least helpful things were.......
◆My strongest feelings were.......
◆In future groups I hope that......
◆One word to describe the leadership was........

PREPARING

Always read through a session thoroughly a few days before you are due to lead it. Gather any props or implements you will need. For every session you will need pens and paper. Other items are listed in detailed notes below.

Think through your responses to the discussion questions.

If you want to read up the background to these sessions these books might help you:
John Drane, **Jesus and the Four Gospels** (Lion, 1984); William Barclay, **The Gospel of Luke** (Daily Study Bible Series) (St Andrew Press, 1975).

It will be helpful if you read Luke's Gospel through yourself. There's a plan on page 29.

RUNNING A SESSION

There is a lot of material in these sessions. But the structure is very flexible and can be used in a number of ways. As with all material of this sort, you are the one in control and it is up to you to choose the activities that will work with your group.

If you use all the material in a session it will take you over an hour.

The aim: Read out the aim, so that everyone knows what you are setting out to achieve.

Warm up: This gets group members relaxed, and raises the subject of the session in a light-hearted way. It should take between five and ten minutes.

Spot check and **Over to you:** After the Bible passage has been read, take about ten minutes on these questions. Spot check questions are deliberately straightforward. If they seem too elementary for your group, create your own questions. Over to you questions are more to do with personal reponses to the passage. The last two are the same every time. Don't miss them out. They give the group a chance to identify the most important elements in the passage for them.

Bible Background: In discussion, especially of the last two Over to you questions, you will be able to point the group to this background to clarify a word or idea in the passage.

Work out 1 (about 20 minutes) **and 2** (about 10-15 minutes): These explore and apply the Bible passage. Usually Work out 1 concentrates on further working with the text; Work out 2 concentrates on applying it at a personal level.

Discussion questions: These are marked ◈ and are dotted throughout the session. Take as long or as little time as you wish on these. They are important, but it's the quality of the discussion, not the length, that determines how helpful it is.

Extra! This is an optional extra to do in the coming week.

SESSION 1

My aim in life: The name is at the bottom, so that each response can be covered up without hiding the person's name. If the members of the group don't know one another, name badges can be a help , and make the activity easier. If the group is large, get into groups of five for this activity.

Work in: Other earlier passages in which Jesus looks forward to these events are Luke 9.21-27 and 44-45.

Protest: Have some copies of your local newspaper handy, so they can see what the letter page looks like.

At the end, remind people to bring to the next session a gift or present they have been given and which they particularly value.

SESSION 2

Gifts: Put the gifts in the centre of the room and number them. Give people only a couple of minutes to guess. That's the least important part of the warm up. The discussion should aim to draw out how it is the relationship with the giver that usually determines how important a gift is to us.

Work in: You could introduce the passage by noting how many important events, e.g. weddings and birthdays, are remembered by special meals. And anything you can do to add to the atmosphere of the reading — lighting or music — would help.

Remember me: Bring some calenders along as examples. Work singly or in pairs, each on one page of the calender. So a small group would do a four-page calender (three months to a page); a larger group could do a twelve-pager (one month to a page). Bring colour supplements and magazines to help with the picture elements — coloured card helps as well.

SESSION 3

Standing firm: These arguments might sound trivial, but don't worry. The activity always works and people shift from the funny to the serious very easily.

Innocent: The idea is to feel both the innocence of Jesus and the injustice of his sentence. The role-play has no parallels to the Bible story. Allow the role-play to run for about three minutes — not more, then ask the characters about their feelings.

SESSION 4

News: You will need a pile of papers for this session. Go through them beforehand, to make sure that stories of the kind that will be useful are there. You are looking for accounts of people doing something out of the ordinary to help others. Ask what today's papers would make of Jesus' death.

Why did Jesus die?: If the group find this difficult, have a large sheet of paper handy. Put up a title "Substitutes". Then "brain-storm" the group for occasions when substitutes are used, e.g. in football, food. Ask what they have in common — someone or something taking the place of another. Can we relate this to what Jesus did?

Once again, you will need magazines to cut up.

Work out 2: You will need to prepare a music tape. Choose two or three different types of songs or music, that express to you some of the meaning of Jesus' death. Some possible examples:

◆ Hallelujah my father for giving us your son, from **Songs of Fellowship,** Kingsway
◆ When I survey the wondrous cross
◆ Adrian Snell — **The Passion**

Ensure that you have the necessary equipment to listen to the music. Ask the group to listen carefully. Afterwards, encourage discussion about what kind of feeling they had as they listened, and what, if anything, the music meant to them.

Extra! This might be an opportunity for God to challenge the group members to commit themselves to him for the first time. If so, you might want to provide a sample prayer or promise for them to use to do this.

SESSION 5

Major event: Be prepared to work with the group at whatever level they choose to operate. How you share the "major event" in your life will, to some degree, set the tone.

In the spotlight: Set up a "Mastermind-type chair", and rig up a spotlight if you can. Each pair has exactly two minutes in the spotlight. Let the group do the cross-examination, but if they need any help you can point them in the following direction:

1. Would the other disciples have made the same mistake? Why didn't the authorities produce the body to silence the disciples?
2. Some of the people who saw Jesus didn't know anyone else had seen him alive. If the disciples had imagined it, why didn't the authorities produce the body to stop the talk?
3. Could Jesus in his weakened state due to wounds and loss of blood, have had the strength to struggle out of the grave wrappings (like being tied up from head to foot), remove the stone, and overcome the Roman guard? And could he then make his way back to the disciples, lie to them, and succeed in giving them the impression that he had conquered death?
4a. This would make the disciples deliberate liars. All they claimed and taught would be based on a known lie. Could such a lie transform their lives and the lives of others in the way that the New Testament indicates that they were transformed?
4b. If the authorities had the body, why didn't they produce it to show that the claims about the resurrection were false?

After discussing the various theories, the question "Why do you think the tomb was empty?", gives the group an opportunity to say where they are.

Work out 2: Give everyone a card showing one of these references: Luke 24.1-12; Mark 16.9-11; Luke 24.13-35; Luke 24.36-49; 1 Corinthians 15.5; John 20.19-23; John 20.24-29; Matthew 28.16-20.

Discussion: Point out that the first Christians were beaten, stoned to death, thrown to the lions dipped in tar and set alight, tortured, and crucified. The empty tomb was a central part of the faith that saw them through that suffering.

SESSION 6

The complete picture: Take three large pictures – e.g. calendar pictures – and cut them up into about ten pieces each, but in such a way that you can cut out a main detail, e.g. a person in the foreground. Keep the pieces with these details on them separate. Then shuffle the rest, and put the pieces into three envelopes. When the jigsaws are complete apart from the missing pieces, get the group to guess what detail is on the missing piece, and then reveal it to them. Finally, draw out some sense of what it feels like when the final piece of a jigsaw drops into place.

Work out 1: Find a range of pictures from magazines and newspapers which you feel would be appropriate for making the posters.

Work out 2: Thank the group for its work. Say what the sessions have meant to you, as well. Remind them of the Luke reading plan and encourage them to read through either that, or the book of Acts.